Answers to Our Everyday Questions
-Volume Three-

Diane K Hiltz Chamberlain

Copyright © 2012 Diane K Hiltz Chamberlain

All rights reserved.

ISBN-10: 151208106X
ISBN-13: 978-1512081060

DEDICATION

As I finish this final volume of "Answers to Our Everyday Questions;" I would like to give thanks and praise, to the One who gave me each word that has been written. Without God's words...there would be no words to write. I remember a time, when I first began my writing and after being published for the first time; I remember thinking to myself...well this is probably all that I am going to have published but after 13 years of ministry work and 16 books; I see a God that is limitless...not only in word but in power and strength. God has truly become the best co-worker a gal could ever ask for; so rather than take the credit for this beautiful book...I give it all back to Him today and thank Him, for all He has done in my life...through my writings and ministry work. I pray that the words within each page will truly touch your heart, as they have mine!

CONTENTS

There are days when I feel as though I'm walking through life alone. How can I know that God is still with me? – pg. 3

My problems have a way of making me feel insecure. What can ease my mind, from these moments of insecurity that make me feel so alone during the difficult times? – pg. 5

I seem to get frustrated over the littlest things. What can help me to find peace, during the overwhelming moments of circumstance? – pg. 7

Why does God allow bad things to happen to good people? – pg. 8

It seems that I hold tightly to guilt and can't let go. How can I rid myself of this tiresome burden? – pg. 10

There are moments when I wonder if God still loves me, due to the failures of the past. How can I know for sure that God has forgiven me? – pg. 11

Why hasn't God responded to my cry for help? How can I find Him, in the midst of all this chaos? – pg. 12

Why is it that I do the things that are wrong, when deep down, I really don't desire to do them at all? – pg. 14

How do I escape moments of temptation? – pg. 16

How do I leave everything with God, when I have so much on my mind? – pg. 18

Why do I tend to get caught up in what I lack, rather than how God can provide for me? – pg. 20

How do I move on with my life and continue to love someone who has come against me? – pg. 21

The Bible says that I'm supposed to forgive others or I won't be forgiven of my own sins. How do I forgive someone who has hurt me so deeply? – pg. 23

I am so overwhelmed by these problems I'm facing. Where is God when I need Him? – pg. 25

For some reason, I tend to put limitations on how far God can work in my life? How can I trust God enough, to let go and allow Him to work in a limitless way? – pg. 27

There are days when I feel as though I can't take one more step forward. How can I find God's strength, during these difficult moments? – pg. 29

I need to feel the presence of God in my life, especially while going through overwhelming moments of circumstance. How can I connect more deeply with God? – pg. 31

Why do I work so hard to be a people pleaser, when there is a God who already accepts me and loves me, for who I am? – pg. 33

I don't know why but I always seem to want to make life work my way. Why is it that I lean on my own thoughts…ways and ideas, rather than

leaning on God? – pg. 34
Why is it that I always seem to be drawn into feelings of discouragement, rather than living with the hope that God will always make a way for me? – pg. 36
Why do I find it difficult to believe that God will always take care of me? – pg. 38
How is it that the moment everything finally seems to be going right; a complete turnaround leads me back into a worse situation? – pg. 39
Why hasn't God answered my prayer? – pg. 41
How is it that I always seem to look for the worst in life, rather than pursuing the best that God longs to offer me? – pg. 43
Can God understand and truly see each tear that is falling within this broken heart? – pg. 44
Why do I feel so bombarded, by the thoughts of a painful past? – pg. 45
Oh God…Satan has me twisted up into a circumstance that I'm not strong enough to get out of. How can I get out of this mess I'm in? – pg. 47
Oh Lord Jesus…how is it that life can seem so difficult? – pg. 49
I've had people walk out of my life, due to my circumstance. Can I really count on God to remain and not walk away? – pg. 51
I took a wrong turn in life. How can I know for sure that God has forgiven me? – pg. 53
You say that Jesus died for me and has now risen and is in Heaven…working on my behalf. If so, then why do I feel as though He has abandoned me? – pg. 55
Why do we race ahead of God and worry about days that haven't even come into existence? – pg. 57
Why do I allow evil to control my thoughts and lead me away from reality? – pg. 59
I try to do my best at life but why is it that I feel that I can't seem to get over the obstacles that stand before me? – pg. 61
How is it that I can be surrounded by people during a difficult time in my life but yet I feel so alone? – pg. 63

INTRODUCTION

Are you living with questions, such as…"Why do I allow evil to control my thoughts and lead me away from reality?" or questions such as…"I took a wrong turn in life. How can I know for sure that God has forgiven me?" or even questions like these… "Oh Lord Jesus…how is it that life can seem so difficult?" and "Why do I feel so bombarded, by the thoughts of a painful past?" "Answers to Our Everyday Questions - Volume 3," will help you to discover God inspired answers, to everyday questions such as these.

"Answers to Our Everyday Questions," by Diane K Hiltz Chamberlain, is her third volume of devotions that are based on the questions we face in life. Are you looking for biblical answers that can lead you into a place of freedom, rather than despair? "Answers to Our Everyday Questions" will do that for you, as you read through 35 devotions that are filled with Bible readings, quotes and God inspired writings…powerful writings that will lead you away from the questions that can trouble your mind.
Come and discover a book of hope that can lead you away from the moments that can weigh you down in life and discover a way to be set free. "Answers to Our Everyday Questions"…along with the Bible can become a powerful tool to cultivate your life and produce lasting growth.
Also…check out volume one and two, of "Answers to Our Everyday Questions!"

THERE ARE DAYS WHEN I FEEL AS THOUGH I'M WALKING THROUGH LIFE ALONE. HOW CAN I KNOW THAT GOD IS STILL WITH ME?

In Joshua 1:9, we read…"Have I not commanded you? Be strong and courageous. Do not be afraid; do not be discouraged, for the Lord your God will be with you wherever you go."

Also, in Psalm 23:4, we read… "Even though I walk through the darkest valley, I will fear no evil, for you are with me; your rod and your staff, they comfort me."

The first thing that can calm our minds and hearts and give us the assurance that God is with us; is that He gives us His promise, through His word; that He will always be with us…no matter what we are going through at the time. We can feel as though we are walking through the darkest valley, when it comes to a circumstance but when we can look for God, through the dense fog of our problems; then we will come to see that He has been there all along.

I remember a time in my own life, when I felt lost in a wilderness of pain and heartache and as I continued to struggle down the path before me; it seemed as though there was only a gray sky, with weeds growing along the pathway. Nothing looked good and I began to feel so alone and destitute, on this path I was walking down, until I began to see that I was too focused on the ugliness of my problems, rather than looking for God in the midst of it all. From there, I began to look for God…lean on Him and allow His words to be etched upon my heart and from that moment on; I knew that I wasn't alone because wherever I walked and whatever I experienced in life; I knew that He was with me.

The thing we need to remember today; is that Satan isn't only out to afflict us but his aim is to put a wedge between us and God; to the place, where we feel abandoned and forsaken by God. The only way we are going to feel God's presence, in the midst of what seems to be a hopeless situation; is to quit sizing up the problem and turn to a great and powerful God…a God that can walk with us…guide us…guard us and protect us, until we have left the storm behind…to walk into the sunshine and beauty of a brand new path.

Quotes: Even though we may feel as though we are walking alone through the darkest valley of circumstance; we can be assured that the light of God's presence is following us behind the clouds.

Safety is not found in the absence of danger but rather safety is found, while seeking shelter in the presence of God.

My problems have a way of making me feel insecure. What can ease my mind, from these moments of insecurity that make me feel so alone during the difficult times?

In Isaiah 41:13, we read…"I am holding you by your right hand—I, the Lord your God—and I say to you, don't be afraid; I am here to help you."

Also in Romans 8:31-32 we read…"What can we ever say to such wonderful things as these? If God is on our side, who can ever be against us? (32) Since he did not spare even his own Son for us but gave him up for us all, won't he also surely give us everything else?" and also in Hebrews 13:6 we read…"That is why we can say without any doubt or fear, "The Lord is my Helper, and I am not afraid of anything that mere man can do to me."

Isn't it amazing how one problem can twist up our thoughts and feelings and make us feel as if we are the only one in the world that is going through a difficult time? While facing these overwhelming circumstances, we can find it difficult to see beyond the horizon of our problem because the problem seems to place us in a web of despair; where all we feel is the control that it seems to have over us at the time. Once we find ourselves caught in this web of despair; all kinds of feelings and thoughts begin to flood our minds, until insecurity begins to set in and take us away from the moments, when we once felt safe and secure with God.

Today, we need to stop looking at where the circumstance has taken us and think on the positive thoughts that remind us of God's love and care for us. We may not be able to actually feel God's grip on us but when we can reflect on Bible verses, such as Isaiah 41:13; then the moments of insecurity will begin to fade into the background, while God's peace becomes a wave that overflows each negative thought and feeling that once had control over us.

We must remember that since God was willing to give up His only Son, as a means of demonstrating His great love for us; then that thought alone should be a reminder; that God's love and presence is greater than any stack of problems that may stand before us. When we can truly understand God's love for us in this way; then we will find it easier to reach out to Him, as a true source of security.

Quotes: Feelings of insecurity enter our lives, when we are more willing to reach out to our problems, rather than to God.

When we are willing to take hold of God's hand during the difficult times; then no source of evil will be able to have its grip on us.

I seem to get frustrated over the littlest things. What can help me to find peace, during the overwhelming moments of circumstance?

In Isaiah 26:3-4, we read… "He will keep in perfect peace all those who trust in him, whose thoughts turn often to the Lord! (4) Trust in the Lord God always, for in the Lord Jehovah is your everlasting strength."

Also, in Hebrews 10:36, we read… "You need to keep on patiently doing God's will if you want him to do for you all that he has promised."

It's so easy to get caught up in the moments that make us feel frustrated and overwhelmed but as I have learned numerous times; falling prey to these moments will never take us anywhere but further down. Satan has a way of not only placing one obstacle in our path but many at one time, until we become overwhelmed and lose the peace that once kept us calm.

When we can keep our thoughts and hearts connected closely to God during the day; then His peace will calm the troubled waters that attempt to overtake us. It's not always easy to separate ourselves from feelings of frustration but when we can find the strength through a powerful God, to look above these moments, rather than face to face with them; then the moments that were attempting to bring us down, will be left behind, as we rise above them, into a perfect peace that can calm any situation.

Today, we need to continue to press on and not allow ourselves to fall prey to these moments that can control our feelings. When we can continue to walk with God…one step at a time, rather than attempting to jam many steps into one; then we will begin to once more experience a peace that can calm any storm.

Quotes: When we turn our eyes upward, in God's direction; then we will be taken above the negative thoughts and feelings that attempt to weigh us down.

The road to perfect peace can only be found, when we are willing to get off the road of frustration and leave anxiety and the overwhelming feelings of life along the wayside.

Why does God allow bad things to happen to good people?

In Romans 5:3-4, we read…"Not only so, but we also glory in our sufferings, because we know that suffering produces perseverance; (4) perseverance, character; and character, hope."

Also, in II Corinthians 4:16, we read…"Therefore we do not lose heart. Though outwardly we are wasting away, yet inwardly we are being renewed day by day."

One thing we need to remember; is to not look at our problems through a worldly eye because when we do this; then we lose hope, rather than seeing the true reason that God has purposed for these difficult moments. When we can shift our thinking and look for the reason, as to why God may be allowing these moments of adversity to enter our lives; then we won't have to ask ourselves the question, as to why bad things happen to good people.

In my own life, I have truly come to discover; that when I look for God's reasoning, rather than focusing on where the problem may be attempting to lead me; then I begin to see that God is using the difficult moments to work at strengthening a weakness in my life that I may not see at the moment. In other words, we become the clay and God becomes the sculptor that is working to rid us of the flaws that may weaken us and keep us from being strong vessels for Him.

I truly believe that bad things happen to good people because God longs to use them in a greater way and sometimes that means that He has to allow weakness to bring us low; so He can rise up in the place of that weakness and make us stronger vessels for Him. I remember a time, when I used to wonder why God allowed so much pain and heartache to enter my life…especially while I was writing and working to serve Him but through time, I began to see that He had a longing to use me in a greater way and in order for me to follow that path; I would have to gain a greater strength for the journey that I was about to face. As I look back to all the times when I said… "Why God," I now see that each weakness I faced was being used out of love, to equip me and prepare me for the moments I now face. Even though we feel as though we are wasting away, due to the trials that enter our lives; we can live with the assurance that each of those moments are being used by God to continually renew us and take us to the next stepping stone that will continually lead us to what He has planned for our lives.

Quotes: The weaknesses in our lives are not meant to harm us but rather they are being used by God to bring us low; so His strength can rise up in their place.

When we can come to see how God can use our weaknesses in a positive way; then we will have a reason to rejoice, rather than to wallow in a pit of weak moments.

It seems that I hold tightly to guilt and can't let go. How can I rid myself of this tiresome burden?

In II Corinthians 10:5, we read…"Casting down imaginations, and every high thing that exalteth itself against the knowledge of God, and bringing into captivity every thought to the obedience of Christ;"

Also, in Hebrews 10:22, we read…"Let us draw near with a true heart in full assurance of faith, having our hearts sprinkled from an evil conscience, and our bodies washed with pure water."

In my own life, I have found that the only way I was able to let go of the heavy burden of guilt, was when I could truly say that I had forgiven myself of past sins. We already know that God is more than able to forgive us but what about ourselves? Have we been able to forgive ourselves, so we can move on with our lives, into the newness that God longs for us to experience?

There are two things that I have discovered about guilt and that is that it can either mean that our consciences are reminding us to let go of a forgiven past or the feelings of guilt can also be used by Satan to remind us of our past failures. Isn't it amazing how Satan can use the past, to lure us into a trap, where he continually reminds us that we are nothing, due to the mistakes of the past?

The only way we are going to be able to rid ourselves of guilt; is when we are able to truly know in our hearts that God is great enough to forgive what we feel can never be forgiven. Once we can accept His free gift of forgiveness…with a complete heart; then we will also be able to forgive ourselves, which will free us from the control of evil, so we can walk in God's newness and leave the heavy burden of guilt behind.

Quotes: Guilt can become a finger that points back at us…only to remind us that we haven't truly forgiven ourselves and let go of the past.

When we allow guilt to take us by the hand and lead us in its direction; we will soon find that we are being led into a trap, where Satan can bring us low, through thoughts and reminders of the past.

There are moments when I wonder if God still loves me, due to the failures of the past. How can I know for sure that God has forgiven me?

In Isaiah 43:25, we read…"I, even I, am he who blots out your transgressions, for my own sake, and remembers your sins no more."

Also, in Philippians 3:13, we read…"Brethren, I count not myself to have apprehended: but this one thing I do, forgetting those things which are behind, and reaching forth unto those things which are before,"

The question we should ask ourselves today; is have we forgiven ourselves. Since God states in His word that He forgives us; then could it be that we haven't let go of the past? If we are ever going to know God's free gift of forgiveness; then we must also be willing to let go and forget the things that once allowed evil to control our lives.

I've often wondered what God must be thinking in the heavens, when we have already asked for His forgiveness; only to return back to the guilt and shame of the past. Do we realize that when we hold tightly to these negative feelings; then we are allowing ourselves to be placed in needless moments of bondage? Instead of listening to the thoughts that attempt to convince us that our past sins are too great for God to forgive; we need to focus on the cross and what it stood for many years ago. If it wasn't for the sacrificial death that Christ experienced at that time; then we would have a reason to question His forgiveness but to think back on a death that not only portrayed forgiveness but love too; should be a reminder to us that He is more than able to forgive us. Let's face it…we are never going to achieve perfection here on earth but when we are willing to let go of the weight of the past and strive for what is awaiting us down the road; then we will come to see that God has truly picked up the pieces of our lives and given us a fresh start.

Quotes: When we question God's forgiveness; then maybe we need to look deep within our hearts, to see if we have forgiven ourselves first.

When we choose to remember a past that has already been forgiven by God; then we are allowing ourselves to be taken to a needless place of bondage.

Why hasn't God responded to my cry for help? How can I find Him, in the midst of all this chaos?

In Psalm 13, we read…"How long, Lord? Will you forget me forever? How long will you hide your face from me?
(2) How long must I wrestle with my thoughts and day after day have sorrow in my heart? How long will my enemy triumph over me? (3) Look on me and answer, Lord my God. Give light to my eyes, or I will sleep in death, (4) and my enemy will say, "I have overcome him," and my foes will rejoice when I fall. (5) But I trust in your unfailing love; my heart rejoices in your salvation. (6) I will sing the Lord's praise, for he has been good to me."

One thing I've always loved about King David; are the moments when he conversed with God, during some of the most trying times in his life. I can't even begin to understand the way he lived and all he went through as king but one thing I have come to understand and relate to; is the way he found God, even in the midst of what seemed overwhelming at the time. If we were to take these verses apart and look for the hidden treasure beneath each line; we would see a man who felt forsaken by God but as he began to pour out the feelings that were attempting to have control over his life; he discovered a way to praise God and dwell on the moments, in which God had been good to him, rather than focusing on where these present moments of difficulty were taking him.

We can be like David and have moments, when we cry out to God and say… "How long Lord? Will you forget me forever?" We can feel as though we cannot find an end, to the wave of circumstance that has brought us to our knees but when we can pour our hearts out to God, rather than trying to remain tough through the storm; then as we release the hurt and pain, of feeling abandoned and forsaken; we will be able to have a clear mind…a mind that will be able to focus on God and how far He has brought us in life, rather than how these moments could possibly defeat us.

There can be times, when it's hard for us to understand, why God doesn't respond to our cries, when we need His help the most but the strength that we can take hold of, during these moments of weakness; is to focus on the One, who can exchange these moments of weakness, for a strength that can lift us to our feet and allow us to keep moving forward, while we wait patiently for God's response.

Quotes: Praising God in the midst of suffering can be the strength that can lift us above our weaknesses.

Focusing on where God has brought us, rather than where our trial is taking us, will bring comfort and hope to our hearts, while we wait for God's response.

Why is it that I do the things that are wrong, when deep down, I really don't desire to do them at all?

In Romans 7:15-25, we read…"I don't understand myself at all, for I really want to do what is right, but I can't. I do what I don't want to—what I hate. (16) I know perfectly well that what I am doing is wrong, and my bad conscience proves that I agree with these laws I am breaking. (17) But I can't help myself because I'm no longer doing it. It is sin inside me that is stronger than I am that makes me do these evil things. (18) I know I am rotten through and through so far as my old sinful nature is concerned. No matter which way I turn I can't make myself do right. I want to but I can't. (19) When I want to do good, I don't; and when I try not to do wrong, I do it anyway. (20) Now if I am doing what I don't want to, it is plain where the trouble is: sin still has me in its evil grasp. (21) It seems to be a fact of life that when I want to do what is right, I inevitably do what is wrong. (22) I love to do God's will so far as my new nature is concerned; (23-25) but there is something else deep within me, in my lower nature, that is at war with my mind and wins the fight and makes me a slave to the sin that is still within me. In my mind I want to be God's willing servant, but instead I find myself still enslaved to sin. So you see how it is: my new life tells me to do right, but the old nature that is still inside me loves to sin. Oh, what a terrible predicament I'm in! Who will free me from my slavery to this deadly lower nature? Thank God! It has been done by Jesus Christ our Lord. He has set me free."

Why is it that we are drawn into the moments that bring sin into our lives, when we have no desire to sin? Why is it that we fall into a trap set up by Satan…one that we have no desire to enter? It's so easy to say that Satan made us sin but that can end up being a cover up, to what may be really wrong. Do we realize that the sin that enters our lives could be due to a weakness that hasn't been resolved? In other words, we can feel as though we have gotten rid of the infested weed; that has attempted to take over our lives but have we left the root of the problem behind; where it can unknowingly grow into something that can create more problems?

Even though we've let go of the old self, when we came to Jesus; it's amazing how the old self can attempt to rise up within us and lead us to sin. When we aren't closely connected to God; then it's as if we have become a sitting target, for evil to enter our lives and have control. The only way we are going to be able to avoid these moments; is when we allow God to exchange these weaknesses for His strength. In other words, we need to look deep within ourselves and see if any root of weakness has been left embedded within our hearts. Once we can acknowledge these weaknesses; then we will be able to open them up to God and allow Him to remove them; so they are no longer able to have control over our lives.

Quotes: When we allow God to dig out the old roots of weakness; then His strength will become embedded within our hearts.

The garden of our hearts will grow and flourish, when we allow God to remove each root of weakness.

How do I escape moments of temptation?

In Matthew 26:41, we read… "Watch and pray that you may not enter into temptation. The spirit indeed is willing, but the flesh is weak."

Also in I Corinthians 10:13, we read… "But remember this—the wrong desires that come into your life aren't anything new and different. Many others have faced exactly the same problems before you. And no temptation is irresistible. You can trust God to keep the temptation from becoming so strong that you can't stand up against it, for he has promised this and will do what he says. He will show you how to escape temptation's power so that you can bear up patiently against it."

Moments of temptation can seem so overpowering, as though we have been captivated within a situation and can't find a way out. We can feel so overwhelmed that we feel that it's easier to give into these moments that are attempting to have control over our lives but we must remember that when we choose to follow Satan's lead; then we are only being led into other moments of weakness, which only makes our situation much worse.

Isn't it amazing how these tempting thoughts can make us feel as though there is no place to escape, from the moments that are attempting to take over our lives? One thing we must do; is to shift our thoughts in God's direction and remember that the power of prayer can move any obstacle that gets in our way. Just speaking the name "Jesus," is powerful enough to throw evil back into hell, where it belongs. The problem we tend to have; is that we become so captivated by what is happening; that we completely bypass the One who can make a way of escape for us. To me, it's as if we are traveling down some unknown road and as we are looking for the right road to take; we begin to get caught up in what is happening around us; to the place where we miss the exit that God wants us to take.

The only way we are going to be able to escape the clutches of temptation; is when we turn to God and allow Him to be our remedy and cure, for these overpowering moments. God never said that we wouldn't face these moments of temptation but He did say that He would make a way of escape for us. We need to realize that the only way we are going to be set free from these moments of temptation; is when we allow God to step in and stomp out the power of evil.

Quotes: Temptation can make us feel as though we are being led down a road where there is no return but when we allow God to walk with us; then

He will make a way of escape.

Temptation only captivates our hearts and minds, when we choose to follow its path.

How do I leave everything with God, when I have so much on my mind?

In Romans 12:1-2, we read…"And so, dear brothers and sisters, I plead with you to give your bodies to God because of all he has done for you. Let them be a living and holy sacrifice—the kind he will find acceptable. This is truly the way to worship him. (2) Don't copy the behavior and customs of this world, but let God transform you into a new person by changing the way you think. Then you will learn to know God's will for you, which is good and pleasing and perfect.

Also in Psalm 55:22, we read…"Give your burdens to the Lord. He will carry them. He will not permit the godly to slip or fall."

The thing that God has taught me, when it comes to leaving everything with Him; is that we also need God to renew our minds, while allowing Him to take us away from the old worldly way of thinking. Before we came to know Christ, we had no powerful source to lean on; so we would worry and panic, the moment a circumstance hit us head on but now that we have invited Christ to come and live within us; we no longer have to lean on weakness because a powerful God lives within us. When we can see God as something stronger than these weak problems we face; then we won't have anything on our minds but Him.

One thing I've always had a difficult time figuring out; is why do we carry our burdens alone, when there is a God that is much stronger…a God that can carry the heavy load for us. We all do this and it seems as though we carry the burden alone, until we become crushed beneath a heavy weight of despair. When we say that we have given our all to God but yet we continue to think on the unfinished business in our lives; then we might as well realize that we never truly gave it all to God.

Today, we need to get alone with God and ask Him to renew us in His Spirit; in a way that will allow us to think on His level, rather than our own. Once we are able to exchange worry, doubt and fear, for a renewed mind; then we will find it easy to give everything to God.

Quotes: A mind that has been totally transformed from a worldly way of thinking will only focus on the things of Christ, while leaving the excess baggage of worry, doubt and fear behind.

When we say that we have given everything over to God but yet we take a few things back; then we are limiting God, as to what He can accomplish in our lives.

Why do I tend to get caught up in what I lack, rather than how God can provide for me?

In Philippians 4:19, we read… "And my God will supply every need of yours according to his riches in glory in Christ Jesus."

Also in Psalm 34:10, we read… "Even strong young lions sometimes go hungry, but those of us who reverence the Lord will never lack any good thing."

Could it be that we are focused more on what we don't have; that we begin to convince ourselves that there is no hope of ever coming through this trying time in our life? It's so easy to get caught up into what we see with our eyes that we find it difficult to go beyond these moments and anticipate something better. How many of us sit and think…well if this doesn't work; then I can do this and make it work, rather than saying…well, I can't make this work but I know a God who can? How long are we going to hold tightly to a rein that we have no control over? Today, we need someone stronger to take care of us and meet these needs and the only One I know of that is powerful enough to replace what we lack is Jesus Christ.

We need to remember that God doesn't always provide by what we think or imagine but rather He provides through His own resources and once we are able to let go and believe in a God who holds the key to so much more than what we lack; then hope will once more spring up within us. Today, we need to believe in a God who can supply our needs according to His riches and once we can truly believe this with all our hearts; then we won't find ourselves so caught up in what we lack.

Quotes: Focusing on what we lack, will only keep us from what we can receive.

Renewed hope will once more lift us to our feet, when we look to God, rather than the problem that stands before us.

How do I move on with my life and continue to love someone who has come against me?

In Matthew 5:43-45, we read… "Ye have heard that it hath been said, Thou shalt love thy neighbor, and hate thine enemy. (44) But I say unto you, Love your enemies, bless them that curse you, do good to them that hate you, and pray for them which despitefully use you, and persecute you; (45) That ye may be the children of your Father which is in heaven: for he maketh his sun to rise on the evil and on the good, and sendeth rain on the just and on the unjust."

Also, in Romans 12:9, we read… "Don't just pretend that you love others: really love them. Hate what is wrong. Stand on the side of the good."

One thing I have come to see within my own life; is when a heart has genuine love for another person; then the hurtful feelings that come our way won't take us down because we will be able to see the reason, for which they came against us, rather than just looking deeply into what they did wrong. I have come to realize that no one ever hurts another person, unless they are hurting first. There has to be a reason behind the hurtful words and pain that one person is afflicting upon another person and if we could just try to see what that reason may be; then we wouldn't have to feel, as though we have been knocked to the ground, by the things that come against us.

In this world we live in…with all its imperfections; the example that is set before us, is to hate those who come against us but when we can separate ourselves from the world and connect ourselves with a God that stands for love; then we will be able to love our enemies and see the importance of praying for them, rather than coming against them, for the wrong they brought against us. I love the reading in Matthew 5:45b, where is says…"for he maketh his sun to rise on the evil and the good, and sendeth rain on the just and on the unjust." In other words, God's love doesn't show any partiality. If we consider ourselves to be true followers of God; then we should also have a love that is more directed towards the need of a person, rather than the wrong that was committed against us. Once we are able to see these difficult moments in this way; then we will gain a new strength from God that will definitely help us to press on with life.

Quotes: A heart of true love will seek out the need of another person, rather than always looking for what is wrong.

When we choose to look for the need of a person who has come against us, rather than looking deeply into the face of what was done wrong; then this means that we have chosen to walk in God's footsteps, rather than our own.

The Bible says that I'm supposed to forgive others or I won't be forgiven of my own sins. How do I forgive someone who has hurt me so deeply?

In Matthew 6:14-15, we read… "For if you forgive other people when they sin against you, your heavenly Father will also forgive you. (15) But if you do not forgive others their sins, your Father will not forgive your sins."

Also, in Matthew 18:21-22, we read… "Then Peter came to Jesus and asked, "Lord, how many times shall I forgive my brother or sister who sins against me? Up to seven times?" (22) Jesus answered, "I tell you, not seven times, but seventy-seven times.

If we were to be honest with ourselves; forgiving someone who has hurt us deeply, isn't always the easiest thing to do. We must remember that our words of forgiveness should always match up with a heart that says to Jesus; that I have truly forgiven the person who has come against me.

If we were to take a look at the life of Christ, we would see someone, who at one time had been loved and followed by many. It was at the cross, where many left their devotion to Christ behind, to reject His ways but through every blow of the whip and every spit upon the face, Jesus still chose to forgive them because His love for them was greater than the wrong that had been done against Him. Are we willing to follow His example? Can we find the strength through Christ, to walk way beyond the fault of another; to love and care for the need, of the one who has come against us? I have come to see that people don't lash out at others for no reason at all. Every bitter feeling and every word of anger is only due to the hurt that they may be feeling within their own life. Can we say that we are perfect, when it comes to moments like these? If we can come to realize that we are frail and weak too; then maybe this will help us to understand…love, and forgive others who may come against us.

Quotes: True forgiveness means that we are able to walk beyond the fault of a person, as though it never existed; to see the need of a heart that needs love, forgiveness and most of all Jesus.

When we focus on the wounds that have penetrated our hearts; then we will never be able to give God a chance to heal what has been torn apart within.

I am so overwhelmed by these problems I'm facing. Where is God when I need Him?

In Psalm 34:18, we read… "The Lord is close to the brokenhearted; he rescues those whose spirits are crushed."

Also, in Jeremiah 23:23-24, we read… "Am I a God who is only close at hand?" says the Lord. "No, I am far away at the same time. (24) Can anyone hide from me in a secret place? Am I not everywhere in all the heavens and earth?" says the Lord."

We all seem to have moments, when we wonder where God is…especially during a time of crisis. One thing I have come to see; is that God is everywhere and in all things. When we touch a flower or walk along a sandy beach at sunset, His presence is there; since He is the One who created all things and continues to control all things. Just think…how could a seed produce a beautiful flower, without His special touch? How could a small bud on a tree limb produce a huge leaf, without His special touch? Who is the One who causes the wind to blow through our hair and who is the one, who paints a different sunset each night? If we would but look…listen and see; we would never have to feel alone, during moments of discouragement because we would always sense the presence of a powerful God around us.

I have come to see that while we are crying out and saying… "Where are you God?"…He is already there. It's us as humans, who build the walls that allow ourselves to feel separated and alone from His presence. With each negative thought and feeling we take in; we are slowly building a wall of circumstance that seems to keep us distant from the presence of God. Rather than taking hold of the problems we face, we need to reach out to the One, who is already standing before us. It's the choices in life that either draws ourselves closer to God or separates us from His presence.

When we can come to see that our God is a god that is closest to us, during the difficult times; then we will always know in the back of our minds that we never have to face another dark and dismal moment alone, which only allows us to feel peace, rather than a longing to look for something we already have.

Quotes: When we focus too much on what is standing before us; then we completely bypass the One who can take us beyond it.

God's presence is only felt, when we invite Him into our thoughts and feelings.

For some reason, I tend to put limitations on how far God can work in my life? How can I trust God enough, to let go and allow Him to work in a limitless way?

In Job 26, we read… "Then Job answered and said: (2) "How you have helped him who has no power! How you have saved the arm that has no strength! (3) How you have counseled him who has no wisdom, and plentifully declared sound knowledge! (4) With whose help have you uttered words, and whose breath has come out from you? (5) The dead tremble under the waters and their inhabitants. (6) Sheol is naked before God, and Abaddon has no covering. (7) He stretches out the north over the void and hangs the earth on nothing. (8) He binds up the waters in his thick clouds, and the cloud is not split open under them. (9) He covers the face of the full moon and spreads over it his cloud.
(10) He has inscribed a circle on the face of the waters at the boundary between light and darkness. (11) The pillars of heaven tremble and are astounded at his rebuke. (12) By his power he stilled the sea; by his understanding he shattered Rahab. (13) By his wind the heavens were made fair; his hand pierced the fleeing serpent. (14) Behold, these are but the outskirts of his ways, and how small a whisper do we hear of him! But the thunder of his power who can understand?"

We all tend to put limitations on God. Is it because we are afraid that we may be disappointed later because God didn't worked in the way we first thought He would or are we finding that we compare His power and strength, to what we see within ourselves and this world? No matter what the reason may be; we are only going to allow the limitless power of God to take over, once we are willing to let go of the reins to our lives and hand everything over to Him.

I love this reading in the book of Job because despite the suffering that Job went through; he focused on the power of God, through what he was viewing around him. Just think…the God that we tend to limit in power; counsels the one that has no wisdom. His powerful presence has stretched one sky across the world, while creating different weather patterns. He is the One that hangs the earth on nothing, while placing boundary lines around the lakes and oceans, so they won't flood the earth. Where is our thinking today? Are we too tightly focused on what is happening around us; that we completely bypass the moments that can lead us to a powerful

God?

If we are ever going to experience a power that goes beyond all boundaries; then first, we need to believe in who God truly is and what He stands for. Once we are willing to look beyond the limitations that we have previously placed on God; then this action alone will open up the complete and fathomless power, of a God that can go beyond what we could ever think or imagine Him to be.

Quotes: When we limit a God that holds within Himself a limitless power; it's as if we have turned off the main power switch to our lives.

We will never experience the complete and limitless power of God, until we are willing to get out of the way and allow Him to step in and do the work that only He can do.

There are days when I feel as though I can't take one more step forward. How can I find God's strength, during these difficult moments?

In Isaiah 40:28-29, we read… "Hast thou not known? Hast thou not heard that the everlasting God, the Lord, the Creator of the ends of the earth, fainteth not, neither is weary? There is no searching of his understanding. (29) He giveth power to the faint; and to them that have no might he increaseth strength."

Also, in Philippians 4:13, we read… "for I can do everything God asks me to with the help of Christ who gives me the strength and power."

The first thing we should do is focus on the power of God, rather than the weakness of our circumstance. When we become drawn into what is happening to us, rather than how we can overcome these moments; then we begin to lose strength and feel weak, while we fall beneath the weight of each problem. When we can come to know God, for who He truly is; then we will find His strength available to us whenever we need it. Why do we doubt the strength and power of a God, who not only created all things but continues to control all things? Just think…if God was a weak God; then the oceans and lakes would flood the earth and this planet we live on, would no longer be suspended in the heavens. When we choose to focus on the strength that comes from a powerful God; then we will always know that we can make it through whatever stands before us.

Second…we need to shift our thinking away from our own so-called strength and how we can make it on our own. I have come to see, through my own circumstances; that when I tried to lift myself up; then I also completely shut off the power of God in my life, while the load continued to weigh me down; to a place where I wanted to give up.

Today, we need to see that we can only do all things because of the strength that God builds up within us. We also need to realize that the choices and directions we choose to take in life, will either allow God to strengthen us or these choices and decisions will allow the circumstance to take us further down, until all we see before us is a life with no hope. I have come to see that God's strength not only comes about through prayer but also through pursuing His strength. When we can walk beyond a weakness; to pursue a strength that can help us to rise above the despair in our lives; then we will never have to struggle through the difficult moments alone.

Quotes: If we desire God's strength, during a moment of weakness; then we need to quit answering the door to our weaknesses and begin a new, by laying out a welcome mat for God… outside the door of our hearts.

When we find it difficult to move on with life, it could be that we are struggling because we are trying to do all things through our own so-called strength, rather than doing all things through a powerful God who can strengthen us.

I need to feel the presence of God in my life, especially while going through overwhelming moments of circumstance. How can I connect more deeply with God?

In Psalm 1:2, we read… "But they delight in doing everything God wants them to, and day and night are always meditating on his laws and thinking about ways to follow him more closely."

Also, in Jeremiah 29:13, we read… "You will find me when you seek me, if you look for me in earnest."

Instead of running to the problem and concentrating on every detail of what is happening in our lives; why not meditate on God and who He really is. I think that many times, we get so caught up in what is happening around us; that we forget to turn to God. I have come to see through my own struggles; that when I run in God's direction and have a good talk with Him; then anxiety is replaced with a perfect peace that will not only calm me down but will also draw me closer to God, in a much more personal way.

Also, we need to have daily talks with God. Bowing our heads and praying to God is good but I have found that when I get alone with God and have a personal talk with Him, as though He is in the room with me; then my connection with Him seems to be much deeper. Talking with God not only connects us with Him but it also gives us a chance to get all of the negative thoughts and feelings off of our chest and one thing I can truly say about these personal moments with God; is that we could never find a better friend that is more than willing to listen to us.

Many times, I think that we struggle, when it comes to having a close knit relationship with God because we don't always have a deep desire to spend time with Him. If we are just running to God, with a to do list and then leaving quickly; only to pursue other things in our lives; then how do we expect to experience a deep and lasting relationship with Him? Look at it this way…if you had a friend and claimed that person to be a good friend but you never gave up some of your own time for this friend; then how would the relationship grow? Well…in a similar way; if we are going to consider God to be a close friend; then we must be willing to pull up a chair within the heart and get to know God, for who He truly longs to be, within each of our lives.

Quotes: Do we truly know God, through a close and lasting relationship or do we just know of Him, by what we have read in His word?

Talking with God in a personal way opens up a clear connection between our heart and His heart; where we are not only able to talk with Him but where we are also able to hear His voice within our spirits.

Why do I work so hard to be a people pleaser, when there is a God who already accepts me and loves me, for who I am?

In Proverbs 29:25, we read… "The fear of man lays a snare, but whoever trusts in the Lord is safe."

Also, in John 12:43, we read… "For they loved human praise more than the praise of God."

Could it be that we are seeking the approval of man, rather than the approval of God? Could it also be that we are so busy looking at the one that is standing before us; that we stop seeking the One that lives within us? These are questions we need to ask ourselves and if we are honest; we may just find that we have our thinking backwards. When we are able to rearrange our priorities and make God first, and then others; then we will always seek to please the One who is at the top of our list.

When we choose to fear what man thinks of us, rather than accepting the love that God already has given us; then we will quickly find that we become a person who is out to please man, rather than God; which only leads us into a snare, where Satan continually controls us and keeps us imprisoned within the work of pleasing others, which only becomes draining and overwhelming.

We must realize today; that there is a difference between loving someone and being so devoted to them; that we end up being unhappy in life, due the standards we have set for ourselves to follow. Once we can discover the real and genuine love that God has for us; then the empty voids within our lives will be filled; to the place where we don't feel the need to please others.

Quotes: When we are able to rearrange our priorities and make God first in our lives; then we will always seek to please the One who is at the top of our list.

When we choose to fear man above God; then we will find that these actions only lead us into a snare that controls us, until we find ourselves pleasing man, rather than God.

I don't know why but I always seem to want to make life work my way. Why is it that I lean on my own thoughts…ways and ideas, rather than leaning on God?

In Proverbs 3:5-6, we read… "If you want favor with both God and man, and a reputation for good judgment and common sense, then trust the Lord completely; don't ever trust yourself. (6) In everything you do, put God first, and he will direct you and crown your efforts with success."

Also, in John 6:63, we read… "The Spirit gives life; the flesh counts for nothing. The words I have spoken to you—they are full of the Spirit and life."

From my own experiences, I have come to see that leaning on one's self, is a way to always be in close contact with the problem. There can be times, when trusting God can seem as though we are slowly walking out into the water…testing it to see if we may fall off the deep end. As we continue to slowly test the waters; we seem to reach a place, where we lose trust and run back to shore.

Today, we need to come to realize that our own thoughts and desires won't count for anything, unless the Spirit of God is attached with them. In other words, we can have thoughts and ideas, as to what we can do, to overcome a situation in our lives but in order for it to work; we must also allow God to work right along beside us. How often do we forget and leave God out of a situation; all because we feel we know what is best for our lives? If we were to think of it in this way; leaning on ourselves only becomes a weak crutch that is about to give way. When we don't turn to God and lean on Him; then the full weight of our problems becomes too much for our own self-made crutch and from there…the crutch breaks, which only causes a fall.

As we face life's challenges, we need a crutch that is strong…a crutch that can hold us up and handle the difficult problems we face. Once we are able to truly trust God and make Him our crutch to lean on, during the difficult times; then the load will become lighter, as a new strength begins to lead us further away from despair.

Quotes: Leaning on God means that we allow the weight of our problems to shift from ourselves, to a God that is strong enough to handle them.

When we choose to lean only, on our own thoughts and desires; then we have left out the One that can crown these efforts with success.

Why is it that I always seem to be drawn into feelings of discouragement, rather than living with the hope that God will always make a way for me?

In Matthew 26: 41, we read… "Keep watching and praying that you may not enter into temptation; the spirit is willing, but the flesh is weak."

Also, in Isaiah 42:16, we read… "And I will lead the blind in a way that they do not know, in paths that they have not known I will guide them. I will turn the darkness before them into light, the rough places into level ground. These are the things I do, and I do not forsake them."

It seems as though we know what we need to do, when it comes to living with the hope that God gives us but to actually follow through with it can be another story. How is it that we believe the words that say that we can make it through a trying time in our lives but yet we find it difficult to follow through with some form of action? One thing I have come to see within my own life; is that we cannot remain idle during a trying time in our lives. No matter how weak we may feel or how discouraged the day may seem; we need to pursue something, other than the feelings of discouragement that is attempting to take over our lives.

When we can come to see that God can lead us through the darkness of a situation; then we will be more likely to take hold of His hand, rather than the hand of our problems. Another thing we need to do, is to turn away from thoughts that tell us that there is no way out of these discouraging moments and begin to truly see God for who He really is, while choosing to believe His word, rather than the thoughts that stem from a circumstance.

I think the reason why we are drawn closer to the feelings of discouragement, rather than clinging to the hope that God gives us in His word; is because we are weak and these weak moments are what draw us like a magnet to evil but one thing we must remember to do and that is to keep watching…praying and anticipating the best that God can bring through a trying time in our lives. When we are able to focus on what can take us further away from the problem, rather than focusing on the problem itself; then our feelings will also go in the same direction as our thoughts and the discouraging moments will be exchanged for a peace that says that everything is going to be alright.

Quotes: When we choose to follow after every negative thought that stems from a problem; then this form of weakness will attach us to evil…like metal to a magnet.

Our circumstance may allow us to feel as though we are blind, while walking through a dense fog of uncertainty but when we choose to trust God and take hold of His mighty hand; then He will lead us away from the obstacles that can cause a fall.

Why do I find it difficult to believe that God will always take care of me?

In Philippians 4:19, we read… "And it is he who will supply all your needs from his riches in glory because of what Christ Jesus has done for us."

Also, in Luke 12:6-7, we read… "Are not five sparrows sold for two pennies? And not one of them is forgotten before God. (7) Why, even the hairs of your head are all numbered. Fear not; you are of more value than many sparrows."

I think the first thing we need to do; is quit visualizing how God will care for us. In other words, we need to just let go and let Him do what He has promised He would do. I think that sometimes, we put too many stipulations on how God will meet our needs and then when things don't work out, in the way we imagine them to happen; then we grow discouraged and want to throw in the towel altogether.

The second thing we need to remember; is that God cares for us through His own resources and when we can see Him as a God that has control over all things; then we won't find ourselves focusing on the details of how this should happen or how that should happen. When we attempt to figure out, how God will do this or do that in a certain way; then unknowingly, we put limitations on what God can do, rather than allowing Him to do all that He longs to do within our lives.

When we can come to truly believe the words of Psalm 112:7b-8, which reads… "…for he is settled in his mind that Jehovah will take care of him. (8) that is why he is not afraid but can calmly face his foes;" then we will be able to go on with life and know in our hearts; that no matter what we face; God will be there to take care of us.

Quotes: When we limit God, as to how we think He will care for us; then later we find that we lack some of the benefits that we need from Him, to help us during a time of need.

When we can completely trust God to meet all our needs; then we find that we lack nothing in life.

How is it that the moment everything finally seems to be going right; a complete turnaround leads me back into a worse situation?

In Matthew 12:45, we read… "Then it says, 'I will return to the man I came from.' So it returns and finds the man's heart clean but empty! Then the demon finds seven other spirits more evil than itself, and all enter the man and live in him. And so he is worse off than before."

Also, in James 1:2-4, we read… "Consider it pure joy, my brothers and sisters, whenever you face trials of many kinds, (3) because you know that the testing of your faith produces perseverance. (4) Let perseverance finish its work so that you may be mature and complete, not lacking anything."

Life as a Christian always seems to be a battle. We can feel as though we are on a high one moment, while the next moment leads us back down into a pit of despair. Why is it that this happens? I have come to see over time; that being a Christian means that we will always face battles in life because we are striving to remain committed to God and because of this; Satan is always working overtime, to devise some form of affliction that will take us permanently out of commission with God.

The thing we need to remember today; is that these moments of ups and downs doesn't mean that it's always due to sin but rather, we can also be experiencing a battle between good and evil…a battle that is after our soul. When Satan sees that we have overcome one thing; it's his job to go back and bring even more into our lives; so that we will become weaker…to the place where we will give in and give up on God.

Rather than focusing on all the problems that seem to be hitting us head on; we need to focus on how God can use them to strengthen us and bring about better things in our lives, so we won't become so vulnerable to Satan's attacks. When we can view our trials with a joyful heart, rather than a heart of dread; then we will begin to take our focus away from the difficult moments that stand before us; while will begin to look at how God can use the trial, to produce new growth and a greater strength that can help us to once more rise above the difficult moments in our lives.

Quotes: We mature spiritually, when we work our way up through the weaknesses, to discover a greater strength than our own…a strength that can only be found through Jesus Christ.

When we can look for something good through a difficult situation; then instead of falling down; we will find that we are being lifted up through the circumstance, as God begins to increase our strength through the weakness.

Why hasn't God answered my prayer?

In Ecclesiastes 3: 1, 11, we read… "There is a time for everything, and a season for every activity under the heavens: (11) He has made everything beautiful in its time. He has also set eternity in the human heart; yet no one can fathom what God has done from beginning to end."

Also in Mark 11:24, we read… "Therefore I tell you, whatever you ask for in prayer, believe that you have received it, and it will be yours."

Two things that I have come to see, when it comes to answered prayer; is are we willing to wait for God's timing and do we truly believe in what we ask for? Let's look at God's timetable, as a puzzle that is slowly being put together. First, we must consider that there may be things in our lives that God longs to do through our moments of affliction; so if He was to allow the pieces of our lives to be put quickly into place before the right time; then maybe we will only see the results but not actually experience what He longs for us to learn and understand. Through my own moments of affliction; I have come to see that God's timing is always right. When we choose to walk in sync with God and trust Him, as we go through life's experiences; then we not only see what He is longing to teach us but we also learn to go in His direction and lean on Him, rather than the problem.

Once we are willing to wait on God…no matter how difficult the moments may appear to be; from there we must look deep within our hearts and see if we truly believe in what we ask Him for. In other words, are we praying…only to walk away and go back to the wallowing hole of our problems or are we walking away with a heart that is waiting for God to work, as we anticipate what He is about to do? We need to remember that the way we react to our prayers, either shows God the true desire of our hearts or words that hold no meaning. I have come to see that whatever I pursue; that is what I will receive. I remember a time, when I would pray and ask God for help but then go back and get upset and say…
"Well…what's next?" From there, I quickly learned to keep my mouth shut and meditate on God, rather than what was standing before me. It's so easy to allow our thoughts to take us away, to a place where we see our prayers, as only a chance to talk with God and give our needs to Him but we must remember that what follows our prayers; is either going to become wings that transport our needs to God or empty words that only fall to the ground. Once we are able to truly seek and pursue our hearts desires, rather than using our prayers, as a time to just talk with God; then we will find that we have opened up some space within our hearts, where God can feel

that He is welcome, to begin a great work within us.

Quotes: When faith and belief are attached to our prayers; then they become wings that transport our needs to the throne of God.

When we choose to wait for God to put each piece of our lives back together; we can be assured that each piece will fit perfectly back into place.

How is it that I always seem to look for the worst in life, rather than pursuing the best that God longs to offer me?

In II Corinthians 4:18, we read… "So we do not look at what we can see right now, the troubles all around us, but we look forward to the joys in heaven which we have not yet seen. The troubles will soon be over, but the joys to come will last forever."

Also, in Psalm 34:14, we read… "Turn away from evil and do good; seek peace and pursue it."

Many times, we can get dragged away from the presence of God and what He longs to do within our lives because we are deeply involved in what is happening around us. We must remember that the things we are experiencing in this life are only happening for a short time; even though these circumstances and problems we face can attempt to convey a different message to us.

When we are able to remove our focus away from what is seen and begin to pursue the things that haven't yet come to pass…the things that God longs to offer us through these difficult moments; then we will begin to feel as though hope is once more sprouting up within us. We might as well realize today; that when we allow evil to lead us into the dark and unknown moments of our thoughts; then these will become the moments, when we find ourselves easily led astray; to a place where we only experience the worst in life.

If we are truly longing to pursue God's best, rather than always looking for the worst in life; then we need to focus on the positive things that can lead us to a good outlook on life. We will only find life difficult and draining, when we choose to follow the negative thoughts that take us away from the presence of God, while leading us into the unknown territory of evil.

Quotes: When we are able to leap over an obstacle of circumstance and move forward in life; then we will find ourselves aiming for the prize, rather than succumbing to defeat.

The direction we're headed in will be based upon who we choose to follow.

Can God understand and truly see each tear that is falling within this broken heart?

In Psalm 56:8, we read… "You have seen me tossing and turning through the night. You have collected all my tears and preserved them in your bottle! You have recorded everyone in your book."

Also, in Psalm 126:4-6, we read… "May we be refreshed as by streams in the desert. (5) Those who sow tears shall reap joy. (6) Yes, they go out weeping, carrying seed for sowing, and return singing, carrying their sheaves.

The tears of a broken heart can make us feel alone and sometimes abandoned by God and we can even question God, as to whether He truly understands and sees the painful tears that fall from within. As I experienced many painful moments in my life; I came to see that the tears that fell like rain within my heart, were actually touching God's heart too, since He lives within my heart. One thing we must remember; is that God's Son, Jesus Christ, was the first to understand rejection, pain and deep heartache; so why do we doubt or question Him, when it comes to understanding our needs and broken hearts?

Sometimes, I think that if we were to enter God's warehouse, where He has stored all our tears; then we would truly see how much He has cared for us. Just think…every painful moment and every tear that has fallen, has been recorded. I would think that if He didn't care; then He wouldn't go to such great measures to understand each need that we face in life.

When we can connect with God; whose heart is greater than any other heart we may come in contact with; then we will never face doubts, as to whether God cares for us or not. Even though the long nights of pain and heartache can seem to have no end; we can rest assured that God will use each tear to refresh and renew us, while leading us into the joy of a new morning.

Quotes: Our tears become a language to God, when our hearts are too broken to speak.

The tears of a broken heart become a gentle rain that refreshes and renews us; so the presence of God's light can once more shine again.

Why do I feel so bombarded, by the thoughts of a painful past?

In Ephesians 6:12, we read… "For we wrestle not against flesh and blood, but against principalities, against powers, against the rulers of the darkness of this world, against spiritual wickedness in high places."

Also, in James 4:7, we read… "Submit yourselves therefore to God. Resist the devil, and he will flee from you."

I remember many times in my past, when Satan continually filled my thoughts with painful memories, due to a past sexual abuse. I would experience flash backs and it seemed as a though I was constantly being reminded of all that took place but over time, I came to see that this was just another one of Satan's tactics, to keep me in a wallowing hole of despair and distant from what God truly longed to do, through these difficult moments.

We must remember that until a weakness in our lives has been strengthened through God; then these moments of the past will continually be used against us by evil. Satan may not be able to prey on the strengthened areas of our lives but he definitely has a way of working on weakness.

Today, we must learn to submit ourselves to God, during these difficult times and resist what Satan is attempting to do. Yes…we need to deal with the past but we should never walk this path alone. Instead, we need to take hold of God's hand and allow Him to walk us out of these moments of weakness and lead us safely; to the place where we can be strengthened and find freedom from the past.

We already know that Satan is going to bombard our thoughts, due to a form of weakness that has been left behind…weakness that hasn't been dealt with but when we can lean on a strong God and exchange these moments of weakness, for a greater strength that can only be found through Jesus Christ; then we will have shut off the three-way connection, between us…our problem and evil.

Quotes: When we choose to hand over our weaknesses to God and exchange them for His great strength; then the power of evil will no longer have anything to prey on.

When we choose to submit ourselves completely to God during the difficult times; then we will reap His benefits of peace, love and a sustaining spirit.

Oh God…Satan has me twisted up into a circumstance that I'm not strong enough to get out of. How can I get out of this mess I'm in?

In John 8:32, we read… "Then you will know the truth, and the truth will set you free."

Also, in Galatians 5:1, we also read… "For freedom Christ has set us free; stand firm therefore, and do not submit again to a yoke of slavery."

First of all, we need to slow down and gather our thoughts together and see what we are focusing on. If we are deeply involved with the problem…especially when it comes to fixing the problem on our own; then we will only continue to be twisted up within the problem, until Satan has full control. From there, we need to shun the deceptive thoughts that Satan is using, as a means of luring us away from the truth and what is actually taking place at the moment. We also need to give the problem completely over to God and stop running the show on our own; so we can work with Him and allow Him to untangle us, from the mess we seem to be in.

We need to realize that Christ has already freed us through the cross and even though there may be moments, when we fall prey to a problem; Christ's death…blood and strength, is more than able to remove us from these difficult moments. The problem I think we all face; is that we get so caught up in how we think the problem needs to be resolved; that we push God out completely, until we panic and fall beneath the weight of the problem.

When we are able to relax and let go of the problem and trust Christ completely, while truly believing in the freedom for which He died for; then we will be able to experience a powerful strength that Christ alone can only offer us…a strength that can go to work and untwist us from these difficult moments of despair.

Quotes: When Satan attempts to twist us within a knot of problems; it's good to know that God's strength is strong enough to unravel us from each problem.

God's truth becomes the key that unlocks the door of deception and sets us free.

Oh Lord Jesus…how is it that life can seem so difficult?

In John 16:33, we read… "I have told you all this so that you will have peace of heart and mind. Here on earth you will have many trials and sorrows; but cheer up, for I have overcome the world."

Also, in I Peter 1:7, we read… "These trials are only to test your faith, to see whether or not it is strong and pure. It is being tested as fire tests gold and purifies it—and your faith is far more precious to God than mere gold; so if your faith remains strong after being tried in the test tube of fiery trials, it will bring you much praise and glory and honor on the day of his return."

Jesus never promised that life would always be easy but He did say in His word that He would be with us and that He would use these difficult moments to make us stronger…that is if we are willing to allow Him to do so. I remember reading an article, on the purification of gold and did you know that when they test gold with fire; that all the impurities float to the surface, where they can easily be removed? Even though our lives can have moments, when we feel as though we are on a roller coaster, while one day may be up and one day down; we can rest assured that God has not forsaken us but rather, He is at work…refining us into something stronger and more precious in His sight.

One thing that has been of comfort to me, while going through many difficult moments in my life; is when I reflect on who God is and not only His power but how He remains undefeated in this world. When we can look beyond the daily problems and focus on an undefeated God; then we will be able to grasp onto a piece of hope that will hold us up and keep us moving forward in life.

Jesus never said that we wouldn't experience trials and moments of pain and sorrow but He did tell us that because He had already overcome these things; that we could live with the hope that a time would come, when we would be able to walk away from the pain and heartache; to experience something new…something we never experienced before. When we are willing to allow God to refine us and remold us through a trial, rather than fighting Him; then and only then, will we come to see the true and undefeated God we serve.

Quotes: Life becomes difficult, when we view it through a worldly eye but when we choose to view our circumstances through God's eye; then we will find that a new outlook on the problem stands before us.

The moments when we walk through the fire of testing can seem painful but when we allow God to hold our hand and walk us through the fire; then we find that the trial becomes less painful, as we begin to see how God is working, to bring us out of the fire, as something brand new.

I've had people walk out of my life, due to my circumstance. Can I really count on God to remain and not walk away?

In Deuteronomy 31:8, we read… "It is the Lord who goes before you. He will be with you; he will not leave you or forsake you. Do not fear or be dismayed."

Also in Psalm 139:8-10, we read… "If I ascend up into heaven, thou art there: if I make my bed in hell, behold, thou art there. (9) If I take the wings of the morning, and dwell in the uttermost parts of the sea; (10) even there shall thy hand lead me, and thy right hand shall hold me."

We can experience hurtful moments, while walking down a dark road of circumstance…moments that make us feel alone and even abandoned by God but even though others come against us or walk away, we can hold to the promises that God gives us in His word; that He will never leave us alone, during the difficult times.

How is it that we compare God to man? Is it because we have been so deeply hurt by man that we begin to see God in the same light? We must remember that when we have God living within us; then our hearts contain a love that is much different and unconditional; compared to the untrusting and fragile love we experience here on earth. If we were to read the promises that God gives us in His word; then we would see that His love holds no limitations. God's love walks beyond the problem, to look for the need of the heart and with a love that great, we can count on God to never walk away.

Today, what we need to do, as a means of putting our minds at ease; is to focus on the words in the Bible that says that God will never leave us or forsake us, instead of focusing on the deceptive lies that attempt to convince us that God doesn't care. When we can come to believe these promises; then we will always look for God's presence…no matter what we are facing or no matter where we are in life.

Quotes: Our circumstances can make us feel as though we are alone on a stormy sea of troubled waters but when we cry out to God for help; we can count on Him to walk out on the stormy waters and be with us, until the storm passes by.

Others may walk away and never return, during the difficult times but we can count on God to walk through the rubble of our problems and meet us at the need of our heart.

I took a wrong turn in life. How can I know for sure that God has forgiven me?

In Isaiah 1:18, we read… "Come, let's talk this over, says the Lord; no matter how deep the stain of your sins, I can take it out and make you as clean as freshly fallen snow. Even if you are stained as red as crimson, I can make you white as wool!"

Also, in Ephesians 2:1-5, we read… "And you were dead in the trespasses and sins (2) in which you once walked, following the course of this world, following the prince of the power of the air, the spirit that is now at work in the sons of disobedience— (3) among whom we all once lived in the passions of our flesh, carrying out the desires of the body and the mind, and were by nature children of wrath, like the rest of mankind. (4) But God, being rich in mercy, because of the great love with which he loved us, (5) even when we were dead in our trespasses, made us alive together with Christ—by grace you have been saved—"

It's amazing how we believe that what seems to be the worse sin, can never be forgiven. I truly believe that Satan is behind this and he is out to convince us that nothing is powerful enough to forgive us…so we can let go of the wrong that we have committed and move on with life. I have come to see that one of Satan's greatest tactics is to keep us in a pit of despair; where we feel unloved…unforgiven and totally abandoned by God but if we were to journey back, to an old rugged cross; we would see a man that not only died for the sins of this world but a man that took upon Himself, every sin that we would commit in this life. With every blow of the whip…that became one more stripe upon His body that paid the price for all sin.

We must remember that Jesus not only died for the little things that would go wrong in our lives but for all sin and His death made a way to cleanse and remove each stain from our lives; that came about by evil. We need to realize that even though we may be a Christian…we still remain in an imperfect world and there may be times, when we fall prey to our weaknesses, as Satan uses them against us, as a means of attempting to remove us from the presence of God. One thing we must never do; is fall prey to hopelessness, while choosing to believe the deceiving lies that Satan attempts to convince us of. Instead, we need to walk back to an old rugged cross and allow Jesus' blood to cleanse us and remove each stain of sin from within us; so that we are able to walk away, in steps of newness. When we choose to run to God, rather than to the sin that is attempting to take over our lives; then we will know without a doubt that we have truly been forgiven.

Quotes: The stain of sin can only be cleansed from within us; when we choose to apply the blood of Jesus Christ to the stain of sin.

Forgiveness only happens, when we choose to allow Christ to wash us and cleanse us deep, from the embedded stain of sin. When we allow Him to work in this way, then we will come out of the wash…white as wool and the stain will be permanently removed.

You say that Jesus died for me and has now risen and is in Heaven…working on my behalf. If so, then why do I feel as though He has abandoned me?

In John 15:16, we read… "You did not choose me, but I chose you and appointed you so that you might go and bear fruit—fruit that will last—and so that whatever you ask in my name the Father will give you."

Also, in John 14:18, we read… "No, I will not abandon you or leave you as orphans in the storm—I will come to you."

And in Matthew 28:20b, we also read…"and be sure of this—that I am with you always, even to the end of the world."[b]"

The first thing we need to remember; is that God chose us first and displayed a true and lasting love for us, when He gave His only Son, Jesus Christ, to die out of love, for the sins of this world. Let's ask ourselves a question today. Why would Jesus go through such a brutal death, as a means of showing His love and forgiveness to us…just to walk away and abandon us? We must remember; that Jesus' death was not any ordinary death but it became the complete sacrifice for our sins. In other words, Jesus became the lamb and His cross became the alter; for which He gave up His entire life…out of a true and lasting love for us; that we may live with forgiveness and a hope that would allow us to press on in life, rather than remain in a pit of destruction.

The question we should ask ourselves today; is have we accepted God's free gift of love and forgiveness or have we been listening to our problems and daily struggles, while we allow them to manipulate our thoughts and feelings? Satan seems to be constantly devising ways to convince us that God no longer loves us and has abandoned us and once we choose to believe these deceiving lies; then that is when our thoughts are driven away from the true love that God has for us; which only allows us to feel abandoned by Him.

Today, we need to focus on the cross and continually be reminded of a love that was so real…a love that we could never experience, in any other way. Once we come to truly accept the love that God is offering us; then the feelings of loneliness and abandonment will become a thing of the past.

Quotes: When we allow our attention to be snagged by deceiving thoughts; then we will be led astray, to a place where we feel abandoned by God.

When we come to see that God chose us first; then we will never doubt His love, which will always keep us closer to Him and further away from the problem.

Why do we race ahead of God and worry about days that haven't even come into existence?

In Genesis 16:1-4a, we read… "Now Sarai, Abram's wife, had borne him no children. But she had an Egyptian slave named Hagar; (2) so she said to Abram, "The Lord has kept me from having children. Go, sleep with my slave; perhaps I can build a family through her." Abram agreed to what Sarai said. (3) So after Abram had been living in Canaan ten years, Sarai his wife took her Egyptian slave Hagar and gave her to her husband to be his wife. (4) He slept with Hagar, and she conceived. When she knew she was pregnant, she began to despise her mistress."

Also, in Genesis 21:8-10, we read… "Time went by and the child grew and was weaned; and Abraham gave a party to celebrate the happy occasion. (9) But when Sarah noticed Ishmael—the son of Abraham and the Egyptian girl Hagar—teasing Isaac, (10) she turned upon Abraham and demanded, "Get rid of that slave girl and her son. He is not going to share your property with my son. I won't have it.""

In these Bible readings today, we think back to the story of Sarah, Abraham and Hagar, which is a prime example of what can happen, when we race ahead of God. As Sarah grew impatient with God; she decided to move ahead on her own, rather than waiting for God to act and in the end; she experienced deep heartache, due to the decisions she made in haste.

Why is it that we attempt to enter days that do not exist and how is it that we don't know which direction to take in life but yet we still move ahead on our own without God? Maybe it's because worry has led us down this unknown path or maybe we just don't want to worry, so we speed ahead and try to figure everything out in advance and fix the situation on our own.

This morning, as I was getting around, I was thinking about this writing and I found myself saying to God… "I have no reason to think about how this or that is going to work out in the days ahead but rather I just need to focus on what is before me." You know…when we choose to react to life in this way; then we will have no need to worry or move ahead on our own because God will be right on the other side of us; where we can converse with Him moment by moment, as He leads us into new days that were created…just for this specific moment in time.

Inspiring Quotes: When we fall out of sync with God; then we are entering territory that may be unknown to us but not to Satan.

When we attempt to enter days that haven't come into existence; then we become distant from God, while we draw closer to unknown problems....which from there, only leads us to needless suffering.

Why do I allow evil to control my thoughts and lead me away from reality?

In Genesis 3:1-5, we read... "Now the serpent was more crafty than any of the wild animals the Lord God had made. He said to the woman, "Did God really say, 'You must not eat from any tree in the garden'?" (2) The woman said to the serpent, "We may eat fruit from the trees in the garden, (3) but God did say, 'You must not eat fruit from the tree that is in the middle of the garden, and you must not touch it, or you will die.'" (4) "You will not certainly die," the serpent said to the woman. (5) "For God knows that when you eat from it your eyes will be opened, and you will be like God, knowing good and evil."

Also in Matthew 4:8-11, we also read... "Again, the devil took him to a very high mountain and showed him all the kingdoms of the world and their splendor. (9) "All this I will give you," he said, "if you will bow down and worship me." (10) Jesus said to him, "Away from me, Satan! For it is written: 'Worship the Lord your God, and serve him only.' (11) Then the devil left him, and angels came and attended him."

One of Satan's greatest tactics is to remove us from reality and paint a picture of our lives that just doesn't exist, as a means of controlling us; while keeping us from working with God, on the problems that need to be resolved within our lives. When Satan can lure our thoughts, into believing that nothing is wrong; then the problem remains and he continues to have control over our thoughts, feelings and the way we react to life.

I remember a time in my life, when I came to finally accept that I had been sexually abused. Isn't it amazing how we can suppress the pain and hurt in our lives, while we bury reality deep inside of us; where we can walk away and not have to deal with the problem? The only thing wrong with this; is that other roots begin to sprout from the main root of the problem, which only leads us to further problems, until we fall beneath a heavy load that is too heavy for us to bear.

When we choose to come to a place in our lives, where we are able to truly hand our problems over to God, rather than burying them deep within us; then and only then, will we be able to live in the light of reality, where darkness cannot imprison us and lure us into an unreal world.

Inspiring Quotes: When we choose to bury reality deep within us, while we live in an unreal world; then a day will come, when reality begins to surface and have control over our lives, from where it left off.

When we allow evil to control our thoughts; then we will only be led in a direction that takes us into an unreal world of pain and heartache.

I try to do my best at life but why is it that I feel that I can't seem to get over the obstacles that stand before me?

In Psalms 144:1, we read… "Bless the Lord who is my immovable Rock. He gives me strength and skill in battle."

Also, in Proverbs 19:21, we read… "Many are the plans in a person's heart, but it is the Lord's purpose that prevails."

The first question we should ask ourselves today is this… "Are we taking God into battle with us and allowing Him to work through us, as a means of overcoming the obstacles that are blocking our path?" If we were to stop and think on the words we speak, we would find that the word "I" seems to get in the way of the word "God." It's amazing how our words can lead us in a different direction; then what God has planned for the moment; which only makes our situation much more frustrating.

Even though God has given us minds to think and make plans, we should always allow His purpose, to prevail above our own, during these difficult moments. Over time, I have come to see that when I gather my plans and ideas together and turn them over to God and let Him decide, as to how I can overcome an obstacle in my path; then I know that I can trust His final decision, to be the answer that can free me and help me to rise above the obstacle that seems to be having control over my life.

We might as well realize that these obstacles that Satan places in our path are much too big and heavy for us to handle on our own but when we choose to let God enter our path and work with us; then we won't have to be frustrated over an obstacle that just won't move because a God that is rich in power and strength, is more than capable of lifting these obstacles from our path.

Inspiring Quotes: When we attempt to remove an obstacle from our path alone; it's as though we are chiseling away at something that is too big for us to handle but when we are willing to call on a God of great power and strength, during these difficult moments; He will reach down from the heavens and lift the obstacle from our path…while freeing us from what seemed impossible for us to get through.

Handing the reins of our lives over to God, will allow His power to kick in and bring an overwhelming situation to a sudden halt.

How is it that I can be surrounded by people during a difficult time in my life but yet I feel so alone?

In I Peter 5:7, we read… "Casting all your anxieties on him, because he cares for you."

Also, in Deuteronomy 31:8, we read… "The Lord himself goes before you and will be with you; he will never leave you nor forsake you. Do not be afraid; do not be discouraged."

I remember a time in my life, when I never felt or experienced anything good. It seemed as though the pain and heartache I was experiencing at the time brought me so low that even when I was surrounded by others and my husband Keith; I felt so alone. For the longest time, I couldn't understand these feelings I was experiencing, until God opened my eyes and allowed me to see clearly; that this loneliness wasn't because I didn't have anyone to talk with. Instead, I came to discover that the loneliness I was experiencing; was because I was allowing my problems to have control over me, rather than choosing to connect myself with God. In other words…I was keeping company with a problem, whose aim was to make me feel distant from life and God…a problem that Satan had planned to use against me, so I would give up on life and the things that God longed to fulfill within my life. Once the answer to my question opened my eyes to the truth of what was really happening, I began to work with God; to exchange my weakness for His strength.

It's so easy to get caught up in life's problems, without realizing where they can lead us. We must remember that when we choose to keep company, with any problem we are going through; then Satan is going to use the problem, to make us feel alone and abandoned by God. Even though we can find it so easy to sit and dissect every detail of the problem, we must remember that becoming deeply involved with a problem, is only going to lead us down paths that make us feel lonely and discouraged. When we can find the strength through God; to turn our heads away from what the problem is attempting to convey to us; so we can focus on a God of great strength…love and power; then our connection with Him, will keep us from the dark and lonely moments that can attempt to make us give up on life.

Inspiring Quotes: Having a relationship with life's problems, will only create conflict within our lives and keep us from having a deep and meaningful relationship with God.

When we choose to walk away from God and take hold of a problem, whose aim is to only lead us into darkness; then we will discover lonely moments that draw us into a world of our own…a world that keeps us distant from the presence of God.

Visit Diane at the Risen Hope Ministries…
http://www.risenhopeministries.com

ABOUT THE AUTHOR

DIANE K HILTZ CHAMBERLAIN

Diane K Hiltz Chamberlain is the author of 16 books, which range from devotionals, to quotes and poetry...to the story on her life..."Baby Steps: A Journey with God through a Lifetime of Pain and Heartache."

All of Diane's books have been written from a heart that has overcome many painful moments of circumstance. As each weakness was exchanged for the perfect strength that God could only offer Diane; a new heart began to break through the calloused moments of the past; so God could use what Diane had been through, as a means of reaching out to others in despair.